Birthday wishes for you

The Lord bless you and keep you and make his face shine on you and be gracious to you.

Numbers 6:24-25

YOUR growth

CHART according to me!

Grow in the grace and knowledge of Jesus. 2 Peter 3:18

All about you

The Lord has made today.
So rejoice and be glad.
Psalm 118:24

your favorite...

activity............................

holiday............................

game...............................

outing.............................

color..............................

smell..............................

book...............................

dessert............................

room...............................

body part..........................

song...............................

dream car..........................

friend.............................

memories from the PAST

May the Lord turn his face toward you and give you peace.

Numbers 6:26

For I know the plans I have for you," declares the Lord, "plans to prosper you and not to harm you, plans to give you hope and a future. Jeremiah 29:11

Rating your Skills

On how you...	☹ ☺ 😊
Fix things	
Sing	
Dance	
Clean	
Cook	
Listen	
Give hugs	
Make others happy	
Home-care	
Play	
Care for others	
Learn new things	
Gardening	

For we are God's handiwork, created in Christ Jesus to do good works, which God prepared in advance for us to do. *Ephesians 2:10*

If there was a movie about YOU

It would be

Visit our website www.iCharacter.org for more great kids books and downloads.

www.iCharacter.org

Published by iCharacter Limited ®. (Ireland)
By Agnes de Bezenac
Illustrated by Agnes de Bezenac
Copyright 2020. All rights reserved.
www.iCharacter.org

Copyright © 2020 by iCharacter Limited ®. All rights reserved. No part of this book may be reproduced in any form or by any electronic or mechanical means, including information storage and retrieval systems, without written permission from the publisher or author, except in the case of a reviewer, who may quote brief passages embodied in critical articles or in a review.